#55
Playa Vista Branch
6400 Playa Vista Drive
Los Angeles, CA 90094

W9-BYI-091

JAN 2 4 2004

Festivals of the World

VIETNAM

Gareth Stevens Publishing
A WORLD ALMANAC EDUCATION GROUP COMPANY

Written by
SUSAN MCKAY

Designed by
LOO CHUAN MING

Picture research by
SUSAN JANE MANUEL

First published in North America in 1997 by
Gareth Stevens Publishing
A World Almanac Education Group Company
330 West Olive Street, Suite 100
Milwaukee, Wisconsin 53212 USA

For a free color catalog describing Gareth
Stevens' list of high-quality books and multimedia
programs, call
1-800-542-2595 (USA)
or 1-800-461-9120 (Canada).
Gareth Stevens Publishing's Fax: (414) 332-3567.

© TIMES EDITIONS PTE LTD 1997
© TIMES MEDIA PRIVATE LIMITED 2001
Originated and designed by
Times Editions
An imprint of Times Media Private Limited
A member of the Times Publishing Group
Times Centre, 1 New Industrial Road
Singapore 536196

Printed in Singapore

Library of Congress Cataloging-in-Publication Data:
McKay, Susan, 1972–
Vietnam / by Susan McKay.
p. cm.—(Festivals of the world)
Includes bibliographical references and index.
Summary: Describes how the culture of Vietnam is
reflected in its festivals, including Tet, the
Firecracker Festival, and the Ngoc Son Festival.
ISBN 0-8368-1937-3 (lib. bdg.)
1. Festivals—Vietnam—Juvenile literature.
2. Vietnam—Social life and customs—Juvenile
literature. [1. Festivals—Vietnam. 2. Vietnam—
Social life and customs.] I. Title. II. Series.
GT4878.5.A2M35 1997
394.269597—dc21   97-8266

2 3 4 5 6 7 8 9 05 04 03 02 01

CONTENTS

It's Festival Time . . .

The Vietnamese word for "festival" is *le hoi* [lay hoy]. A le hoi is usually made up of religious services and lots of fun. Every festival has different ceremonies and traditions. Some are only for members of the family, others include entire cities or villages. No matter what the occasion, you'll find something to smile about. So, let's go! It's le hoi time in Vietnam . . .

WHERE'S VIETNAM?

Vietnam is a long, narrow country shaped something like an "S." It lies in the center of East Asia. About three quarters of the land is covered with mountains. The other quarter has been cut into terraced rice fields.

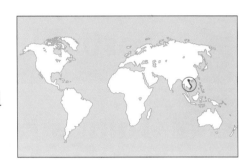

A young Buddhist monk dressed in yellow robes.

Who are the Vietnamese?

The original settlers of Vietnam were farmers who planted grain in the Red River delta. For many years, the Lac Viet, or People of the Valley, as they were called, lived peacefully. But there was always a threat from their powerful neighbors to the north, the Chinese. In 111 B.C., the Chinese invaded and conquered Vietnam. After 1,000 years of Chinese reign, the Vietnamese defeated them.

Today, you may notice that many Vietnamese customs are similar to those of the Chinese. The majority of Vietnamese are descendants of the Viet, Tai, and Chinese migrants who first settled in Vietnam over 2,000 years ago.

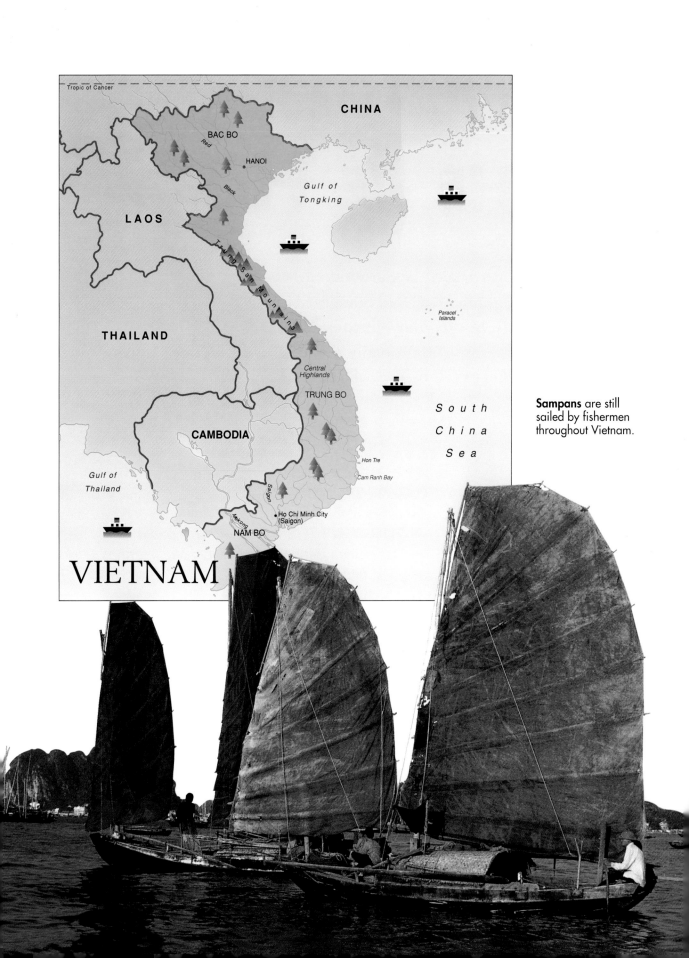

CHINA

BAC BO

Red

HANOI

Black

Gulf of
Tongking

LAOS

Trung Sam Mountains

THAILAND

Paracel
Islands

Central
Highlands

TRUNG BO

South
China
Sea

CAMBODIA

Hon Tre

Cam Ranh Bay

Gulf of
Thailand

Saigon

Mekong

Ho Chi Minh City
(Saigon)

NAM BO

Tropic of Cancer

VIETNAM

Sampans are still
sailed by fishermen
throughout Vietnam.

WHEN'S THE LE HOI?

There are two calendars in Vietnam, one based on the sun (the Gregorian calendar) and one based on the moon (the lunar calendar). In everyday life, most Vietnamese use the Gregorian calendar, the same one you probably use. But the Vietnamese rely on the cycles of the moon to tell them when to celebrate festivals.

Come and cut the rug at the Tet ceremony.

SPRING

- ✪ **LE VAN VUYET DAY**
- ✪ **TET** ✪ **FIRECRACKER FESTIVAL**
- ✪ **HAI-BA-TRUNG DAY**—Celebrates the anniversary of the death of the Trung sisters with parades and festivities.
- ✪ **HOLIDAY OF THE DEAD**—People pay a visit to the graves of their dead relatives and make offerings of food, flowers, and incense.
- ✪ **HO CHI MINH'S BIRTHDAY**

SUMMER

- ✪ **BIRTH, ENLIGHTENMENT, AND DEATH OF BUDDHA**—Birds and fish are set free by Buddhists. In some areas, the birds are trained to put on a show after they have been released.
- ✪ **HUNG-VUONG DAY**
- ✪ **SUMMER SOLSTICE**—People burn paper dolls to satisfy the god of death and put good luck charms by their doors to protect themselves against disease.
- ✪ **WHALE FESTIVAL**—A decorated motorboat carrying a whale altar heads out to sea. After a time, the boat returns and the altar is carried to the temple.

Don't hide under your hat—come on out and celebrate!

AUTUMN

- ✪ **WANDERING SOULS' DAY**—The gates of hell are opened and all the souls fly out. People make food offerings so the souls won't go hungry.
- ✪ **MID-AUTUMN FESTIVAL**
- ✪ **TRAN-HUNG-DAO DAY**
- ✪ **LE LOI DAY**—People celebrate the liberation of Vietnam by the great warrior named Le Loi in the 15th century.
- ✪ **NGOC SON FESTIVAL**
- ✪ **CONFUCIUS' BIRTHDAY**
- ✪ **NATIONAL DAY**

WINTER

- ✪ **HARVEST FESTIVAL**—Children give gifts to their parents, and patients give gifts to their doctors to celebrate the end of the harvest.
- ✪ **TEACHER'S DAY**—Students send gifts to their teachers.
- ✪ **CHRISTMAS**—Special Christmas Day masses are held in Catholic and Protestant churches.
- ✪ **NEW YEAR'S DAY**

7

TET

Tet is Christmas, New Year's, and the fourth of July all wrapped into one. It is the most important holiday in Vietnam. Tet can last anywhere from three days to three months, but in most parts of Vietnam, people celebrate the New Year for about a week.

Burning paper in honor of the kitchen gods.

Showing off new clothes at Tet.

Getting ready

Preparations for Tet start months ahead of time when the streets are lined with stalls selling flowers, food, candles, and clothing. Huge quantities of food are bought, the house is cleaned from top to bottom, and new clothes are set out for everyone to wear on New Year's Day.

The days preceding Tet are also the time when the kitchen gods return to heaven to report on the family. The gods are sent off with a special ceremony. They are good spirits that protect the household. A bamboo pole is erected in front of the house to keep the bad spirits from entering while the kitchen gods are away.

Listen to a story . . .

Long ago, there lived a couple who could not have children. One day, the wife left her husband and ran away. She remarried and had a happy life. Her first husband was so lonely that he went in search of her. When he arrived at her door, she was overcome with pity. She took him in and fed him a meal. It was beginning to grow dark, and she knew her new husband would soon be home from the fields. She hid her first husband under a pile of straw. When her new husband returned, he began to prepare the fertilizer. He set the pile of straw on fire so he could collect the ashes. When the wife realized what had happened, she threw herself into the fire. Her husband was so overcome with grief that he, too, walked into the flames. The Emperor of Heaven was moved by their fate and turned all three into gods to watch over the household. The three kitchen gods are **embodied** in blocks of clay that rest on the cooking pot.

Everyone is happy during Tet. This is not only because it is the festive season; it is also because people are not allowed to fight with one another during the first days of the New Year.

9

Welcome home

The last day before Tet, the streets are empty and the markets are closed. Everyone has gone home to welcome their **ancestors** back. Each member of the family takes a turn bowing in front of the family altar. At exactly midnight, the ancestral spirits arrive. They are welcomed with firecrackers and gunshots. The celebrations continue straight through to the next day.

For children, the highlight of the day is the dragon dance. The dance is like a parade that comes down the street with cymbals clashing and drummers drumming. The costume is made of a papier-mâché mask and a brightly colored silk train. The dragons perform a series of acrobatic feats, so the dancers must be very agile. Sometimes they climb high poles to reach money left for them.

Dragons are symbols of good luck in Vietnam.

Traditional Tet decorations are sold by street vendors.

Superstitions

The Vietnamese have lots of **superstitions** that they associate with Tet. Everything that takes place on the first day of Tet is believed to affect the year ahead.

The first sound on New Year's Day is very important, and everyone tries to detect it above the din of the firecrackers. A cock crowing means hard work and a bad harvest. A dog barking means confidence and trust. A buffalo lowing means a year of sweat.

No housework can be done during Tet because all the good luck might be swept away. No one should fight, get angry, or use swear words, since this will attract the evil spirits. On the seventh day of Tet, the bamboo pole can be taken down because by then the kitchen gods have returned to watch over the households.

Think about this

Like the Scots, the Vietnamese believe the first visitor on New Year's Day will bring all their good or bad luck with them. Happiness and wealth are two very important things to consider when inviting guests to visit at New Year's.

According to Buddhism, monks must wander through the community begging for food. At Tet, the rice **merchants** pour handfuls of rice into the monks' bowls so they can celebrate, too.

FIRECRACKER FESTIVAL

As part of the Tet festivities, a firecracker festival takes place each year in the village of Dong Ky. Firecrackers have always been associated with Tet because during the absence of the kitchen gods, loud noises are used to scare the evil spirits away.

Recently, firecrackers were banned from private use because they can sometimes be dangerous. But firecrackers are still made in Vietnam, and many people believe the ban will not be enough to stop the Vietnamese from celebrating Tet and the Dong Ky Firecracker Festival.

Dancers are flung into the air by an enthusiastic crowd of onlookers.

Opposite: One of the huge firecrackers made especially for the festival.

Continuing the tradition

Each year, 16 families in the small village of Dong Ky in Ha Bac province are chosen to put on a firecracker display. The families spend an entire year and plenty of money preparing for the event. Some families spend up to $500.00 on gunpowder, fuses, and wrapping. This may not seem like much, but for the average Vietnamese family it is a small fortune, more than a year's salary!

The wrapping is usually made of papier-mâché and decorated with animals. Sometimes the firecrackers are so big that it takes as many as 24 men to carry them.

A tripod is set up so the firecracker points toward the sky.

BANG!!!

The highlight of the festival is the procession through the narrow streets of the village. So many people turn up for the event each year, it is sometimes difficult just getting the firecrackers through the alleys. The procession ends at a secluded area where a tripod has been set up. The tripod is used to hoist the firecrackers on end so they point in the air. Once the fuse has been lit, there is an earth-shattering noise and a wonderful display of lights. The bravest men in the village stand as close as they can while the blast occurs. After all 16 firecrackers have been lit, the priests and village elders put their heads together to judge the winner. The family that organized the best display gets a prize!

Think about this
Which day of the year do you set off firecrackers? Do the firecrackers look anything like the ones the Vietnamese make?

Can you hear the loud CRACK as the firecrackers go off?

NGOC SON FESTIVAL

The Ngoc Son Temple lies in the heart of the old town of Hanoi, the capital city of Vietnam. "Ngoc Son" means Jade Mound. The name comes from the temple's location, perched on a tiny island in the middle of a lake. The island is called Jade Island, and it looks something like a mound. Every year, the Ngoc Son Temple holds a festival to honor its three saints and national hero. Many of the temple's worshipers join in the colorful celebration. After a grand procession across the island and a very solemn religious ceremony, there is a great feast. How would you like to come along and take part in the Ngoc Son Festival?

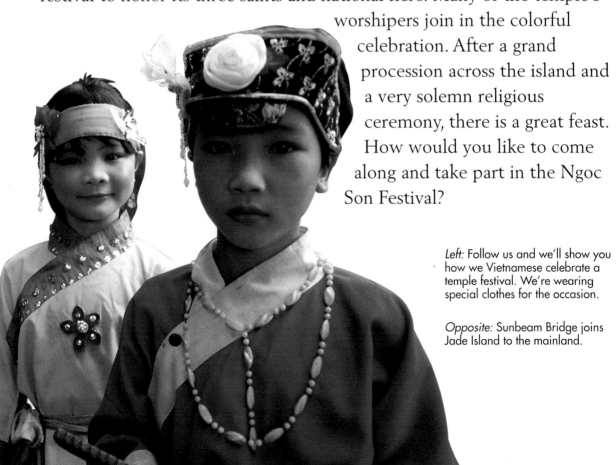

Left: Follow us and we'll show you how we Vietnamese celebrate a temple festival. We're wearing special clothes for the occasion.

Opposite: Sunbeam Bridge joins Jade Island to the mainland.

The procession

Preparations begin long before the actual day. The women of the neighborhood gather together and cook special meals as offerings to the temple's saints and national hero. The Ngoc Son procession starts in the old quarter of Hanoi. The temple is reached from the shore by a brightly painted bridge called The Huc, or Sunbeam Bridge.

Carrying the offerings through the streets of Hanoi.

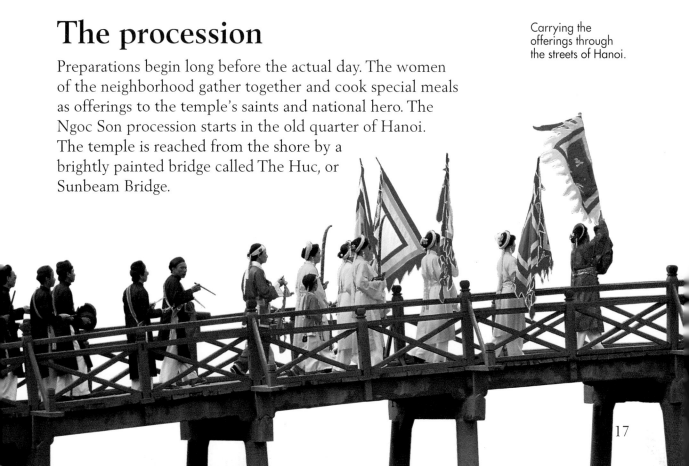

Listen to a story . . .

The Ngoc Son Temple lies in the middle of the Lake of the Restored Sword. The lake and the temple have an ancient legend surrounding them. The legend goes back 500 years. During the days of Chinese domination, the warrior Le Loi received a magic sword from the Divine Tortoise to free the Vietnamese from Chinese rule. After freeing the country, Le Loi (who later became Emperor Le Thai To) took a boat to the middle of the lake to return the sword. The tortoise snatched the sword from his hands and dove down to the bottom of the lake. This is how the lake got its name.

18

Buddhism

The Vietnamese are very religious people. If you go to Vietnam you can see Buddhist temples and pagodas throughout the country. Many of them, such as Ngoc Son Temple, have been built and dedicated to famous people who have served Vietnam. Ngoc Son Temple is dedicated to Tran Hung Dao, a national hero, and three saints: La To, a physician; Quan Vu, a martial arts expert; and Van Xuong, a man who helped develop Vietnamese literature.

Percussion instruments, such as cymbals and drums, are played during the procession.

Buddhism made its way to Vietnam in the second century, nearly 2,000 years ago. Although it came under attack from other religions, such as Confucianism and Taoism, it eventually became the dominant faith. Today, Buddhism is the religion of most Vietnamese.

Opposite, top: Lining up to enter the temple after the procession. Just behind the devotees, you can see the Lake of the Restored Sword.

The Four Noble Truths

Buddhism was founded by a man called Gautama Buddha. He preached the **Four Noble Truths**. He taught people that 1) there is suffering in life; 2) the reason people suffer is because they don't know the truth; 3) by getting rid of selfishness, people won't suffer anymore; and 4) people can perfect themselves by following Buddha's path.

Opposite, bottom: The **vo de cam** [vo duh cam] is a typically Vietnamese instrument. It is a guitar with a long handle, and it usually has three strings. Most vo de cam have a square sound box, but this one is round.

Think about this
Buddha realized the Four Noble Truths while sitting under a banyan tree. Later on, he decided to teach what he had learned to others. Before he died, he had many followers. Today, Buddhism is one of the world's most popular religions.

NATIONAL DAYS

T he history of Vietnam is filled with war and struggle. As early as 111 B.C., the Vietnamese were invaded by their Chinese neighbors to the north. Later, during this century, they fought the French, the Japanese, and the Americans. It was a long, hard battle, but the Vietnamese finally won their independence in 1975. Independence is something the Vietnamese cherish, so they celebrate their freedom through various national holidays.

A portrait of Ho Chi Minh, the father of modern Vietnam.

Selling Vietnamese flags before National Day.

Ho Chi Minh's Birthday

On May 19, the Vietnamese celebrate the birth of their greatest leader, Ho Chi Minh. The day begins with parades through the streets of Vietnam's main cities. Many people carry **placards** of their hero. Later on, there are speeches to remind people of the life of former President Ho.

Ho Chi Minh is often called the father of modern Vietnam. He led the Vietnamese people in battle against the Japanese and the French. In 1945, he set up a new, independent government called the Democratic Republic of Vietnam. But the French army returned the following year. Ho Chi Minh's soldiers fought the French and defeated them in 1954. He died in 1969, in the middle of the war with the United States. Six years later, Vietnam achieved the dream of a unified, independent state.

A parade of women in Vietnam's national dress, the **ao dai** [ow ZAI, in the south, ow YAI in the north].

21

National Day

September 2nd is Vietnam's National Day. This was the date in 1945 when the country achieved independence from the Japanese and the French. The Vietnamese celebrate National Day with parades and singing. Balloons are blown up and carried by enthusiastic marchers. Many people also carry portraits of Ho Chi Minh to honor his memory. (September 2nd is also the anniversary of his death.) It is common to see people dressed in traditional costumes on National Day. These costumes are from the Le dynasty, another time when Vietnam forced out foreign rulers.

Carrying balloons during a National Day parade.

Listen to a story . . .

After years of foreign domination, the people of Vietnam were determined to get rid of the Chinese once and for all. In 1425, a group of men formed under the leadership of a wealthy landowner named Le Loi. Together they organized a resistance movement against the Chinese. As soon as the Chinese heard about the movement, they began arresting the rebels.

Le Loi hid in the mountains and re-grouped his troops. Soon the troops were scoring major victories in battles against the Chinese. China's defeat was so great they were forced to withdraw from Vietnam. Le Loi became Emperor Le Thai To, the founder of the Le dynasty. This is considered Vietnam's Golden Age. Le and his followers promoted Vietnamese art, literature, and education, and protected the rights of the people.

A woman dressed in clothes from the Le dynasty for the National Day parade.

Dragon boats

Dragon boat races on the Saigon River in Ho Chi Minh City.

Dragons are a very important symbol in Vietnam. They are often seen at festivals and celebrations. During the National Day festivities, you are sure to see dragons racing through the river. How is this possible since dragons are mythical creatures? Actually, they are long, narrow boats with the head and tail of a dragon. A drummer sits near the head of the boat and pounds a **tattoo** to help the rowers keep time. Races are held in many of the river ports, and everyone enjoys the fun and excitement.

Think about this
After the long war in Vietnam, many Vietnamese left their country in search of a more peaceful life. Some people went to North America. Others went to Australia and Europe. Overseas Vietnamese are called Viet Kieu in Vietnam.

MID-AUTUMN FESTIVAL

O n the 15th day of the eighth moon (late September or early October), the Vietnamese celebrate Tet Trung-Thu, the Mid-Autumn Festival. This festival honors the moon, which is at its brightest at this time of the year. It is a favorite for children, who dance through the streets carrying lighted lanterns shaped like the full moon, dragons, fish, or rabbits.

A boy stares up in delight at his rabbit lantern.

The mooncake contest

On the day of the festival, the Vietnamese eat special cakes called mooncakes. The cakes are as round as the full moon itself and filled with nuts and fruits. All the girls in the villages compete to make the best mooncakes. In the evening, the cakes are put on display for all to see and taste. Then they are judged by the village elders, and the winner gets a prize.

Children also wear masks to celebrate the Mid-Autumn Festival.

Water puppetry

After the celebrations, many families head off to the lake to watch water puppet shows. Water puppetry is similar to other puppet theater except the puppets don't have a solid stage to perform on. Instead they perform on water. To make the stage, the puppeteers set up screens of reeds on the lake. The screens keep the audience from seeing the puppeteers.

The puppets stand about 2 feet (60 cm) tall and are attached to a small wooden platform. They are moved along the surface of the water with underwater rods that can be as long as 30 feet (9 m). Wires and strings make the puppets come alive.

Many Vietnamese believe the art of water puppetry developed during the long rainy seasons in Vietnam, when everything is covered with water.

Find out how to make a Mid-Autumn mask on page 28.

THINGS FOR YOU TO DO

O ne of the popular games played by Vietnamese children during festivals is O-lang, or Count and Capture. This is a very simple game played by two players. For holes, you can dig hollows into the ground or use paper cups. For counters, you can use any number of things—sunflower seeds, beads, or peanuts.

What you need to play O-lang

Two players face each other across a board. You can make the board from whatever you like, but there must be five holes on either side and one at each end, called the mandarin. Each player starts the game with a total of 35 counters. The players must put 5 counters in each of the holes in front of them, and 10 counters in their mandarin. Now you are ready to begin.

The rules

The object of the game is to win as many counters as you can.

1 One player begins by taking all 5 counters from a cup, and, moving in either direction, dropping one counter in each cup, including the mandarin. The empty cup is now called a pond. As the game goes on, more and more ponds will be created.

2 The aim is to have the last counter land in a cup next to a pond. If this happens, the player collects all the counters from the cup on the other side of the pond. If the player lands in a cup with two consecutive ponds, he does not collect any counters. The lucky player lands next to a pond with lots of counters on the other side.

3 If the player lands in a cup next to a pond that joins a mandarin, the player "eats the mandarin." This means he takes all the counters from the mandarin.

4 When both mandarins have been "eaten," the game is over, and the player with the most counters wins.

Rules to remember

1) You cannot start by picking up counters from the mandarin.
2) Once you have won some counters, be sure to put them aside, away from the board.

Things to look for in your library

The Children of Vietnam. Marybeth Lorbiecki and Paul P. Rome (Carolrhoda Books, 1997).

From Rice Paddies and Temple Yards: Traditional Music of Vietnam. Phong Nguyen (World Music Press, 1990).

Postcards From Vietnam. Denise Allard (Raintree/Steck-Vaughn, 1996).

Tet: Vietnamese New Year. (Best Holiday Books) Dianne MacMillan (Enslow Publications, 1994).

Vietnam. (International Video Network).

Vietnam. (Rainbow Educational Media).

Vietnam: The Land. The Culture. The People. Bobby Kalman (Crabtree Publications, 1996).

MAKE A BASKET MASK

During the Mid-Autumn Festival, Vietnamese children make all kinds of interesting masks. Here's an idea for a mask that you can make to celebrate the moon.

7

6

8

4

1

5

You will need:
1. A basket
2. Elastic
3. Yarn
4. Paper clips
5. Paints
6. Paintbrushes
7. A paint tray
8. A wax pencil
9. Scissors

2

9

3

1 Draw a face on the basket using a wax pencil.

2 Paint in the face.

3 Cut 4-inch (10-cm) lengths of yarn. Divide into two piles. Fold one pile in half and loop through a paper clip. With a smaller piece of yarn, tie the top below the paper clip to be sure it doesn't come undone. Attach the paper clip to the basket. Repeat with the other pile of yarn.

4 Cut a piece of elastic to go around your head. Thread through the basket and tie.

29

MAKE STICKY RICE WITH MANGO

Sticky rice is a common food you'll see at many Vietnamese festivals. Here's a great recipe for a light, refreshing dish that is delicious after a meal or anytime.

You will need:

1. A cutting board
2. 1 cup (225 g) glutinous rice
3. ½ cup (120 ml) coconut cream
4. Measuring cups
5. A wooden spoon
6. ¼ cup (60 g) sugar
7. A sifter
8. 2 mangoes
9. ½ teaspoon salt
10. Measuring spoons
11. A knife
12. A double boiler
13. Water

1 Soak the rice in water for 2 hours. Drain well.

2 In a double boiler, bring water to a boil and steam rice for 30 minutes.

4 Mix the coconut cream, salt, and sugar into the rice.

3 Slice the mangoes lengthwise and remove the seeds.

5 Place rice on a plate and arrange mango slices around it.

31

GLOSSARY

ancestors, 10	Relatives who lived many years ago.
ao dai, 21	Vietnamese national dress. A long dress with slits up the sides worn over pants.
embodied, 9	To be included as a part of something else.
Four Noble Truths, 19	Buddha's solution for the suffering of humankind.
merchants, 11	People who buy and sell goods.
percussion, 19	Instruments, such as drums, cymbals, and tambourines, that are played by striking them with or against another object.
placards, 21	Large cardboard signs carried during marches, parades, and protests.
sampans, 5	Small boats with oars and sails.
superstitions, 11	Belief in magic, ghosts, witches, and devils.
tattoo, 23	A continuous beating on a drum.
vo de cam, 19	A stringed instrument typical in Vietnam.

INDEX